to Aunt [illegible]

from Ruairi
with love

date 12-20-2014

A New Leash on Life

Inspirational Thoughts

rachaelhale

A New Leash on Life

Published by Harvest House Publishers
Eugene, Oregon 97402

ISBN 978-0-7369-2736-9

Design and production by Garborg Design Works, Savage, Minnesota

Printed in China

12 13 14 15 / LP / 10 9 8 7 6 5 4

Become a possibilitarian. No matter how dark things seem to be or actually are, raise your sights and see the possibilities—always see them, for they're always there.

Norman Vincent Peale

Be happy. It is a way of being wise.

SIDONIE-GABRIELLE COLETTE

One of the things I learned the hard way was it does not pay to get discouraged. Keeping busy and making optimism a way of life can restore your faith in yourself.

LUCILLE BALL

To be alive, to be able to see, to walk...it's all a miracle. I have adapted the technique of living life from miracle to miracle.

Arthur Rubinstein

Imagination is more important than knowledge.

Albert Einstein

The greatest discovery of any generation is that human beings can alter their lives by altering the attitudes of their minds.

ALBERT SCHWEITZER

attitude

Happiness isn't about what happens to us—it's about how we perceive what happens to us. It's the knack of finding a positive for every negative, and viewing a setback as a challenge. If we can just stop wishing for what we don't have, and start enjoying what we do have, our lives can be richer; more fulfilled—and happier. The time to be happy is now.

LYNN PETERS

It is our attitude
at the beginning
of a difficult
undertaking which,
more than anything
else, will determine
its outcome.

William James

Character is power.

Booker T. Washington

Far away there in the sunshine are my highest aspirations. I may not reach them, but I can look up and see their beauty, believe in them, and try to follow where they lead.

Louisa May Alcott

The ultimate measure of a man is not where he stands in moments of comfort, but where he stands at times of challenge and controversy.

Martin Luther King Jr.

friendship

By friendship you mean the
greatest love, the greatest
usefulness, the most open
communication, the noblest
sufferings, the severest
truth, the heartiest counsel,
and the greatest union of
minds of which brave men
and women are capable.

JEREMY TAYLOR

A loyal friend laughs at your jokes when they're not so good, and sympathizes with your problems when they're not so bad.

ARNOLD H. GLASOW

Blessed are they who have the gift of making friends, for it is one of God's best gifts. It involves many things, but above all, the power of going out of one's self, and appreciating whatever is noble and loving in another.

THOMAS HUGHES

The only service a friend can really render is to keep up your courage by holding up to you a mirror in which you can see a noble image of yourself.

GEORGE BERNARD SHAW

Whatever is true, whatever is noble, whatever is right, whatever is pure, whatever is lovely, whatever is admirable—if anything is excellent or praiseworthy—think about such things.... And the God of peace will be with you.

THE BOOK OF PHILIPPIANS

Of all the heavenly gifts that mortal men commend,
What trusty treasure in the world can countervail a friend?

NICHOLAS GRIMALD

trusty

A true friend is the gift of God, and He only who made hearts can unite them.

ROBERT SOUTH

Friendship without self-interest is one of the rare and beautiful things of life.

JAMES F. BYRNES

courage

You gain strength, courage, and confidence by each experience in which you really stop to look fear in the face. You are able to say to yourself, "I have lived through this horror. I can take the next thing that comes along."

Eleanor Roosevelt

Your worst days are never so bad that you are beyond the reach of God's grace. And your best days are never so good that you are beyond the need of God's grace.

JERRY BRIDGES

grace

When you get into a tight place where you feel you can't go on, hold on, for that is just the place and the time that the tide will turn.

HARRIET BEECHER STOWE

When one door of
happiness closes, another
opens; but often we look
so long at the closed door
that we do not see the one
which has opened for us.

HELEN KELLER

God stirs up our comfortable nests, and pushes us over the edge of them, and we are forced to use our wings to save ourselves from fatal falling. Read your trials in this light, and see if your wings are being developed.

HANNAH WHITALL SMITH

trials

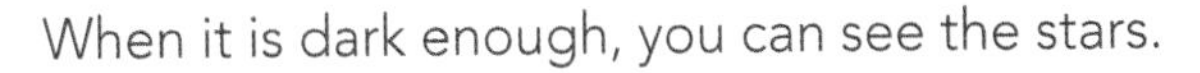

When it is dark enough, you can see the stars.

CHARLES A. BEARD

Good timber does not grow with ease;
the stronger the wind, the stronger the trees.

J. WILLARD MARRIOTT

persist

I will persist until I succeed. Always will
I take another step. If that is of no avail
I will take another, and yet another.
In truth, one step at a time is not too
difficult...I know that small attempts,
repeated, will complete any undertaking.

OG MANDINO

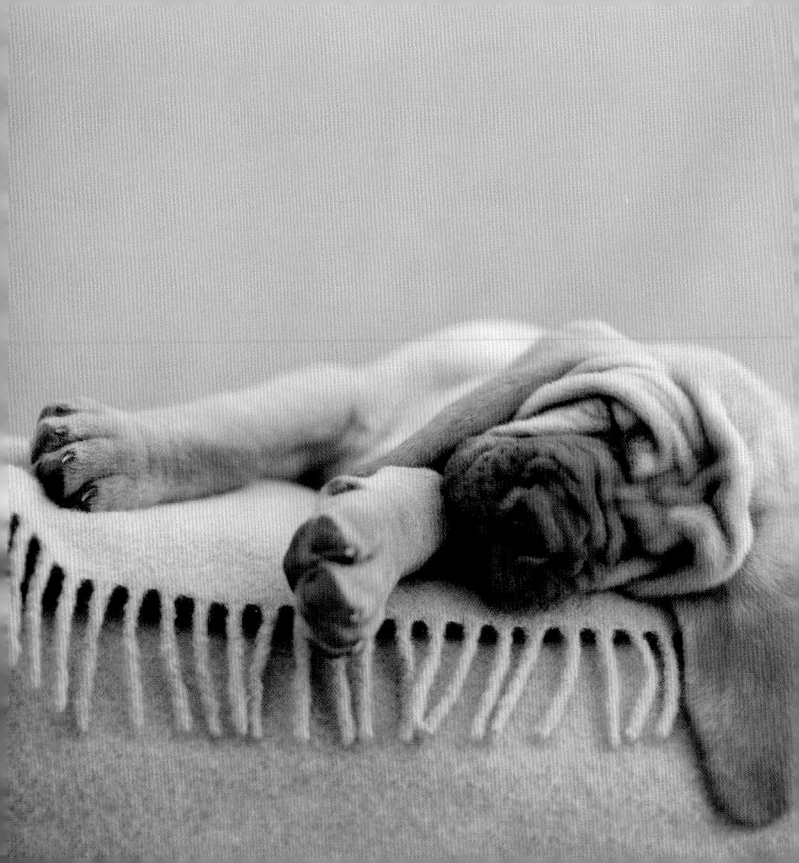

We need time
to dream, time
to remember,
and time to
reach the infinite.
Time to be.

GLADYS TABER

dream

May each day unfold for you like roses,
sparkling in the dew,
that open to the morning sun and bloom
until the day is through.
And may each passing moment bring a song
as pure as angels sing,
but may there be above all things a peace
that only God can bring.

AUTHOR UNKNOWN

Enjoy the successes that you have, and don't be too hard on yourself when you don't do well. Too many times we beat up on ourselves. Just relax and enjoy it.

PATTY SHEEHAN

relax

Happiness is the art of relaxation.

MAXWELL MALTZ

He enjoys true leisure who has time to improve his soul's estate.

HENRY DAVID THOREAU

To be able to fill leisure intelligently is the last product of civilization, and at present very few people have reached this level.

BERTRAND RUSSELL

How far you go in life depends on you being tender with the young, compassionate with the aged, sympathetic with the striving, and tolerant of the weak and the strong. Because someday in life you will have been all of these.

George Washington Carver

Live your life while you have it. Life is a splendid gift—there is nothing small about it.

FLORENCE NIGHTINGALE

Be glad of life because it gives you the chance to love, to work, to play, and to look up at the stars.

HENRY VAN DYKE

Experience is not what happens to you. It is what you do with what happens to you.

ALDOUS HUXLEY

Reflect upon your present blessings, of which every man has many; not on your past misfortunes, of which all men have some.

CHARLES DICKENS

experience

Only those
who dare to fail
greatly can ever
achieve greatly.

ROBERT F. KENNEDY

achieve

Life is no brief candle to me. It is sort of a splendid
torch which I have got hold of for a moment,
and I want to make it burn as brightly as possible
before handing it on to future generations.

GEORGE BERNARD SHAW

The future belongs to those who believe in the beauty of their dreams.

Eleanor Roosevelt

inspiration

We get new ideas from God every hour of our day when we put our trust in Him—but we have to follow that inspiration up with perspiration—we have to work to prove our faith. Remember that the bee that hangs around the hive never gets any honey.

Albert E. Cliffe

You will find as you look back upon your life that the moments when you have really lived are the moments when you have done things in the spirit of love.

HENRY DRUMMOND

Love is a fruit in season at all times, and within the reach of every hand.

MOTHER TERESA

Love is a great beautifier.

LOUISA MAY ALCOTT

If I planted a flower every time I thought of you,
I could walk in my garden forever.

AUTHOR UNKNOWN

For a small child there is no division between playing and learning; between the things he or she does "just for fun" and things that are "educational." The child learns while living and any part of living that is enjoyable is also play.

PENELOPE LEACH

play

To live exhilaratingly in and for the moment is deadly serious work, fun of the most exhausting sort.

BARBARA GRIZZUTI HARRISON

It is a happy talent to know how to play.

RALPH WALDO EMERSON

fun

We don't stop playing because we turn old, but turn old because we stop playing.

AUTHOR UNKNOWN

We may run, walk, stumble, drive, or fly, but let us never lose sight of the reason for the journey, or miss a chance to see a rainbow on the way.

GLORIA GAITHER

chances

Keep on going and the chances are that you will stumble on something, perhaps when you are least expecting it. I have never heard of anyone stumbling on something sitting down.

CHARLES F. KETTERING

Become an answer to someone else's prayer. Visit a sick relative or friend, call someone and encourage them, mow a neighbor's yard, give your spouse a back rub, write a check for a local charity, compliment a coworker, volunteer at a shelter for the homeless. Lift your spirits by lifting someone else's load.

TRACY MULLINS AND ANN SPANGLER

God doesn't send them because we deserve it. He sends them because we need help. Angels are literally messengers of God's mercy.

MAC HAMMOND

What lies behind us and
what lies before us are
tiny matters compared
to what lies within us.

RALPH WALDO EMERSON

Consider it pure joy...whenever you face trials
of many kinds, because you know that the
testing of your faith develops perseverance.

THE BOOK OF JAMES

I try to avoid looking forward or backward,
and try to keep looking upward.

CHARLOTTE BRONTE

The difficulties we experience always
illuminate the lessons we need most.

AUTHOR UNKNOWN

That's what it takes to be a hero, a little gem of innocence inside you that makes you want to believe that there still exists a right and wrong, that decency will somehow triumph in the end.

LISE HAND

innocence

Life at its best is a series of challenges. A big enough challenge will bring out strengths and abilities you never knew you had. Take on your challenges and you will bring yourself to life.

AUTHOR UNKNOWN

Don't go through life,
grow through life.

ERIC BUTTERWORTH